Football Friends
A Game for Everyone

By Michael Hennebry

Today is a big day! Little feet run fast.

We're all here to play football, at last!

The ball is round, big and bright.

We kick it left, we kick it right!

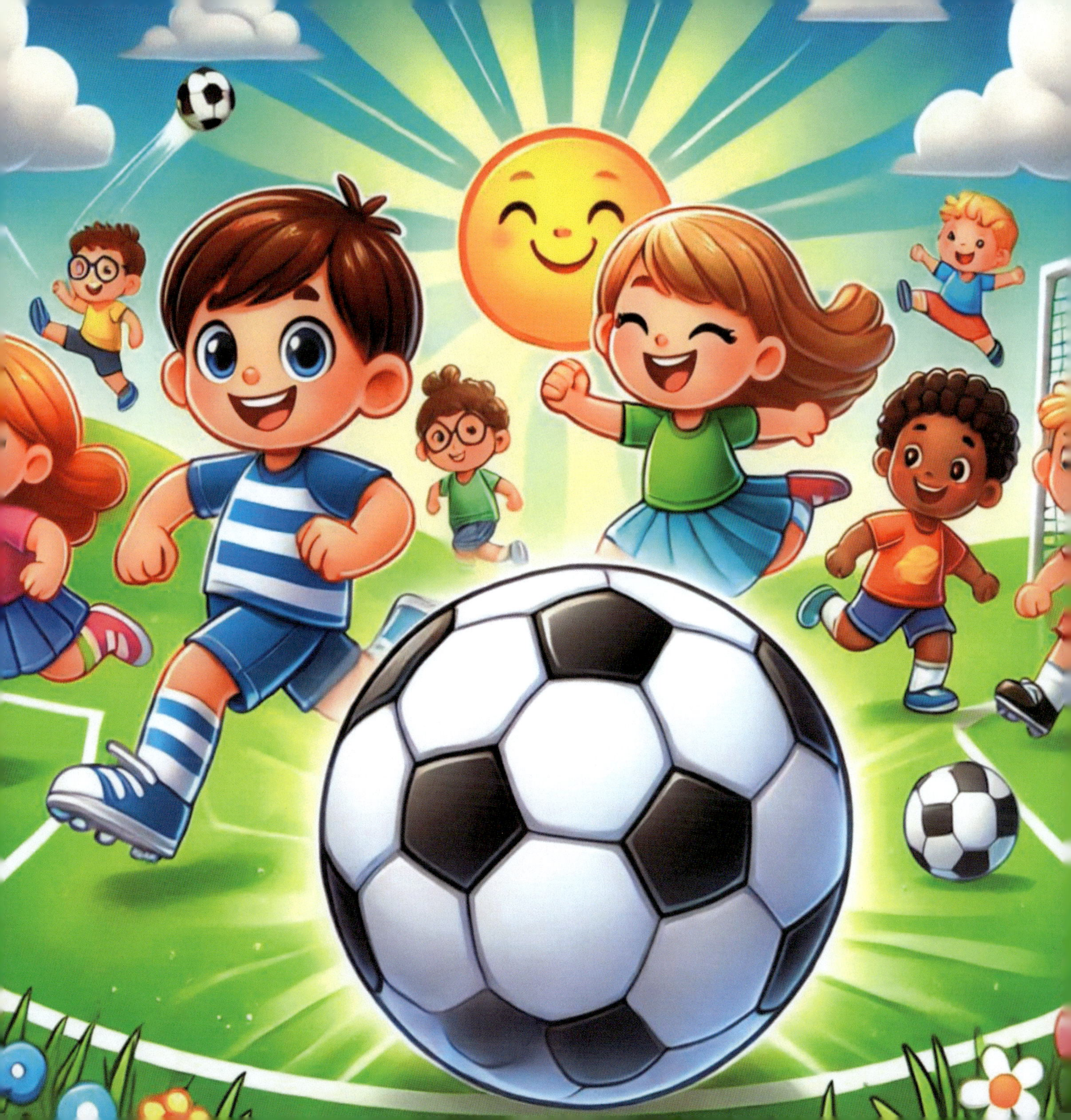

Look at all the kids around.

Different faces, different sounds.

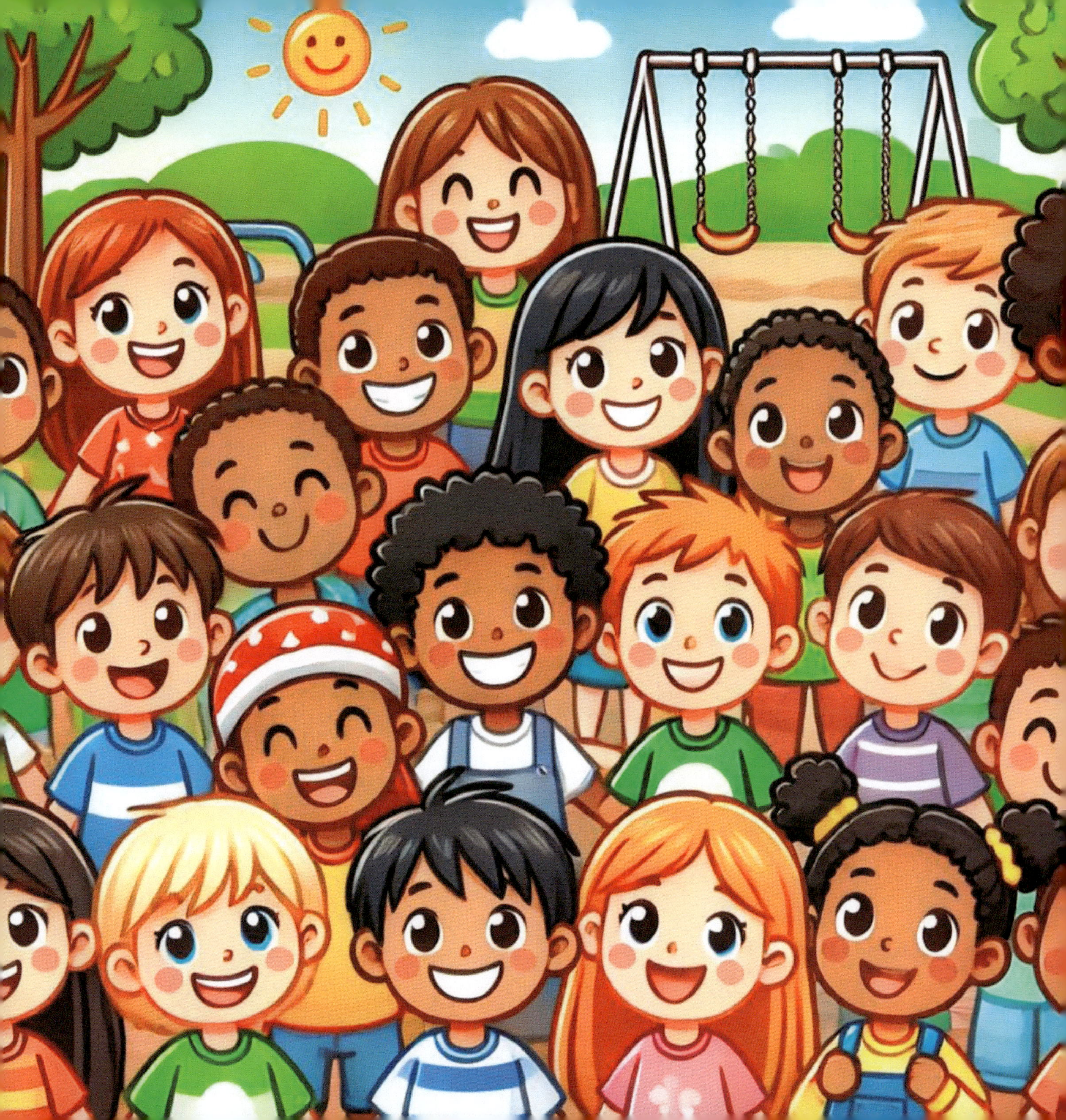

Some kids are big, some kids are small.

But football is a game for us all!

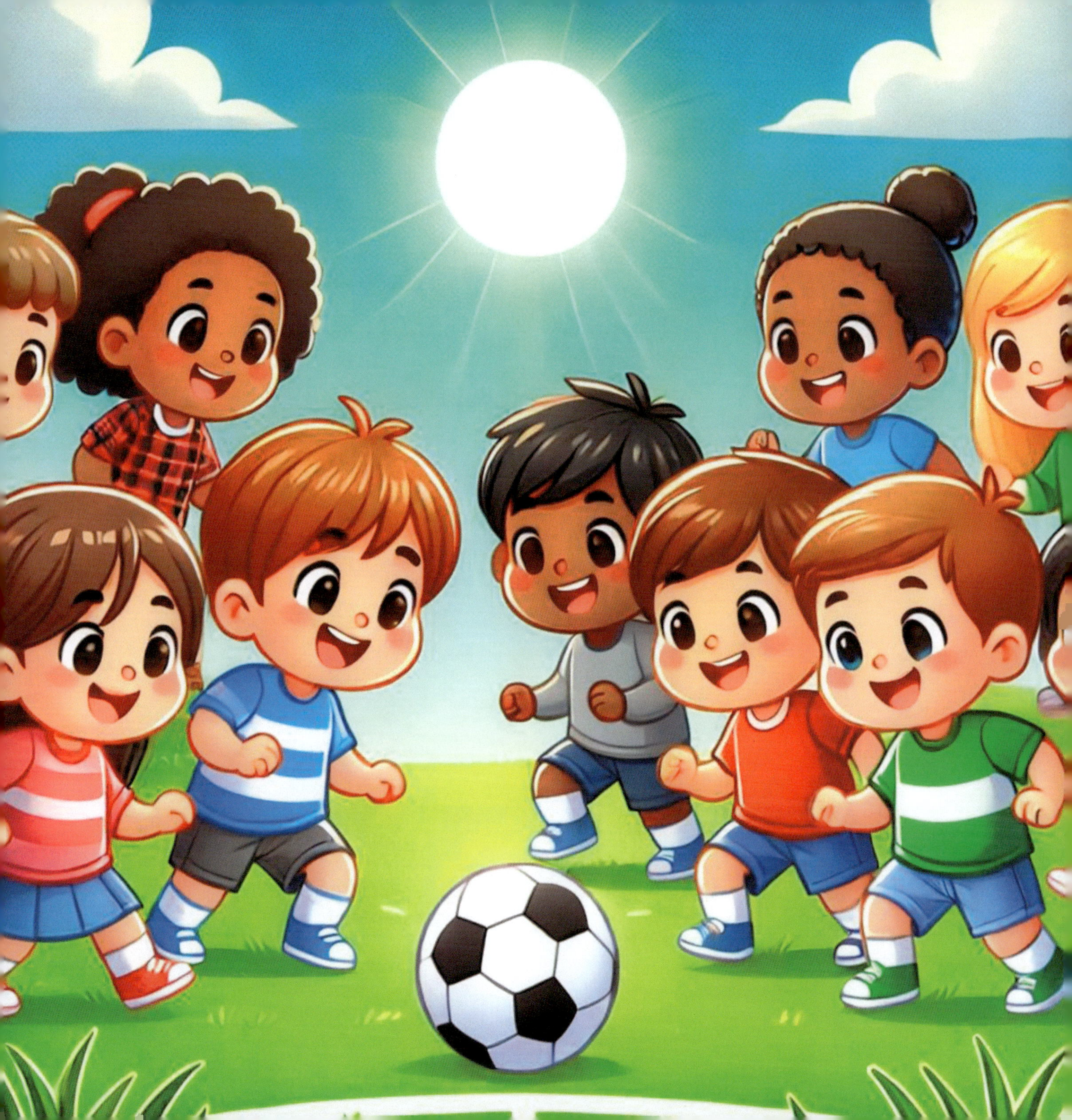

Juan kicks the ball, so strong and high.

It zooms through the air, up to the sky!

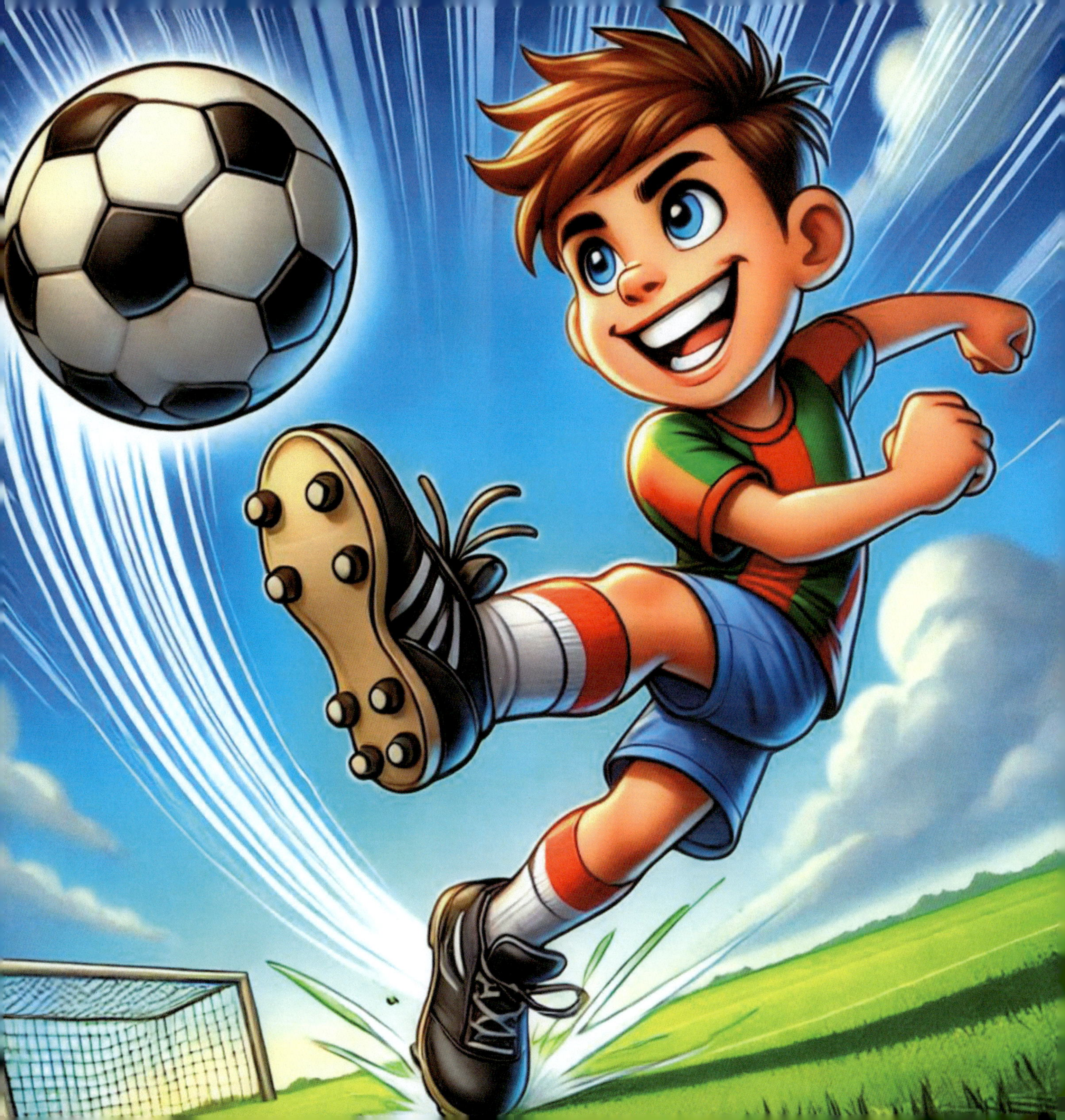

Then Aisha kicks with a happy cheer.

The ball comes down, and rolls so near.

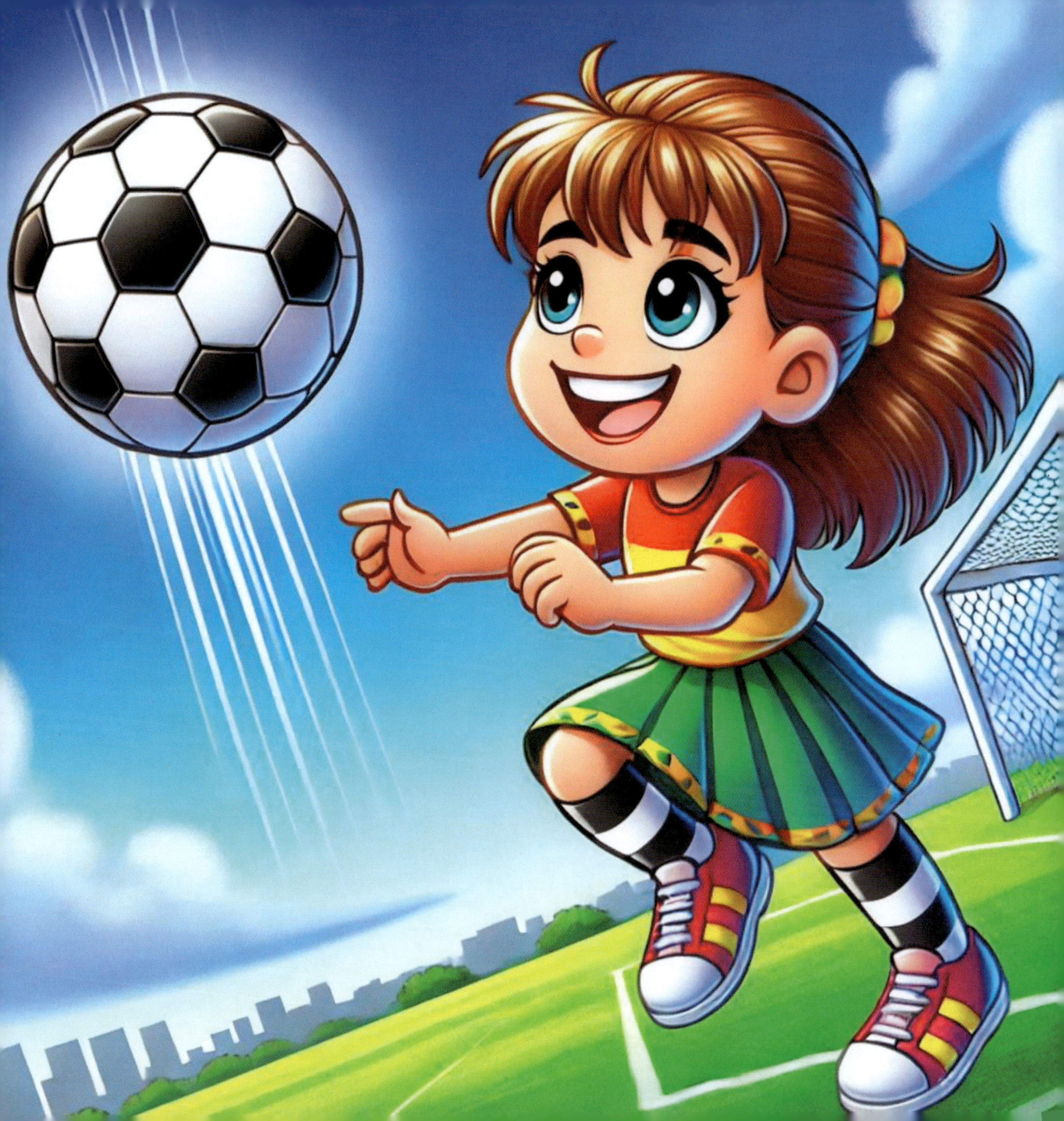

Lin smiles wide and gives it a tap.

All our feet go pat-pat-pat!

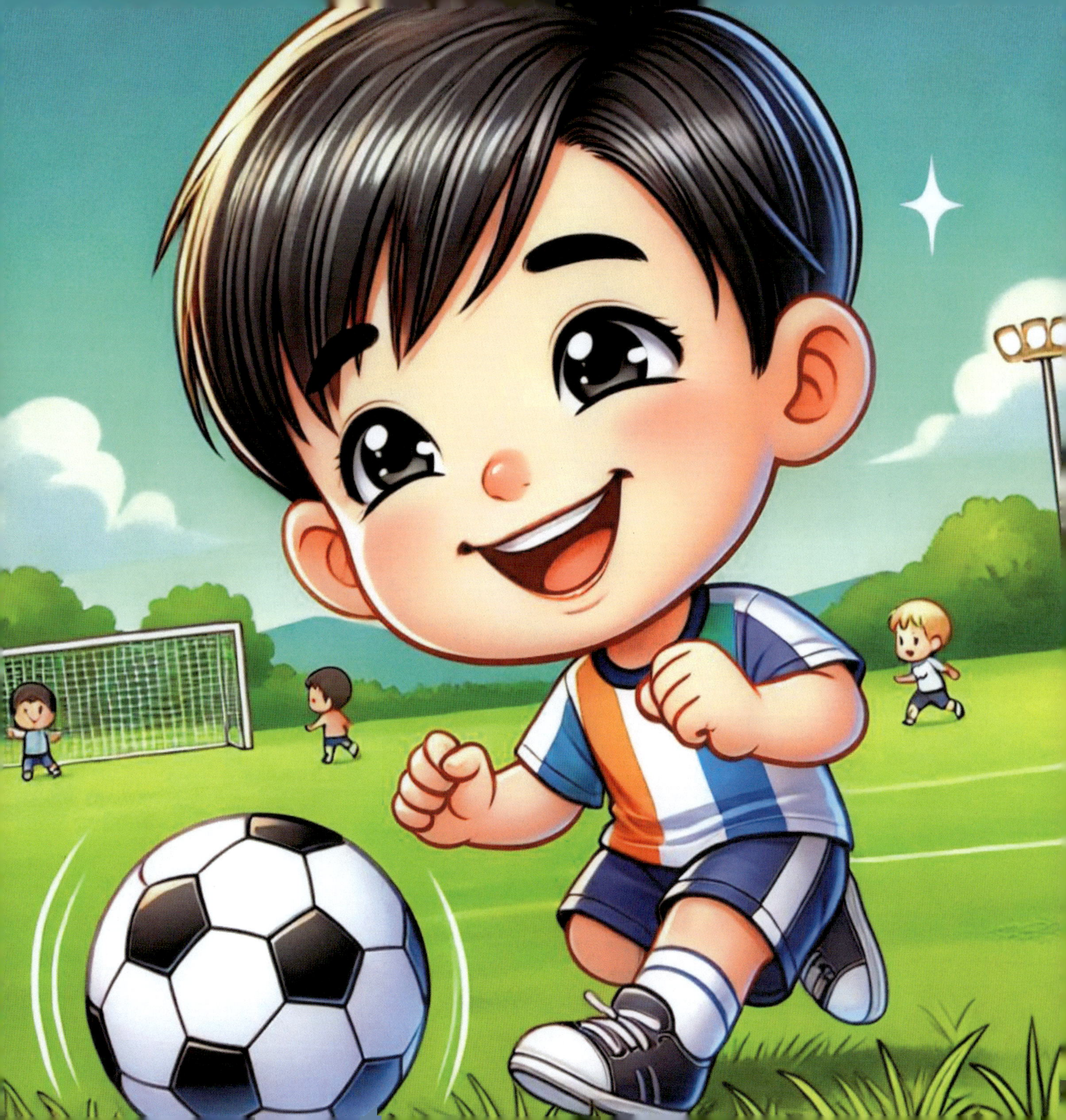

We don't need to say a word, not at all.

Our feet and the ball do the talk—they call!

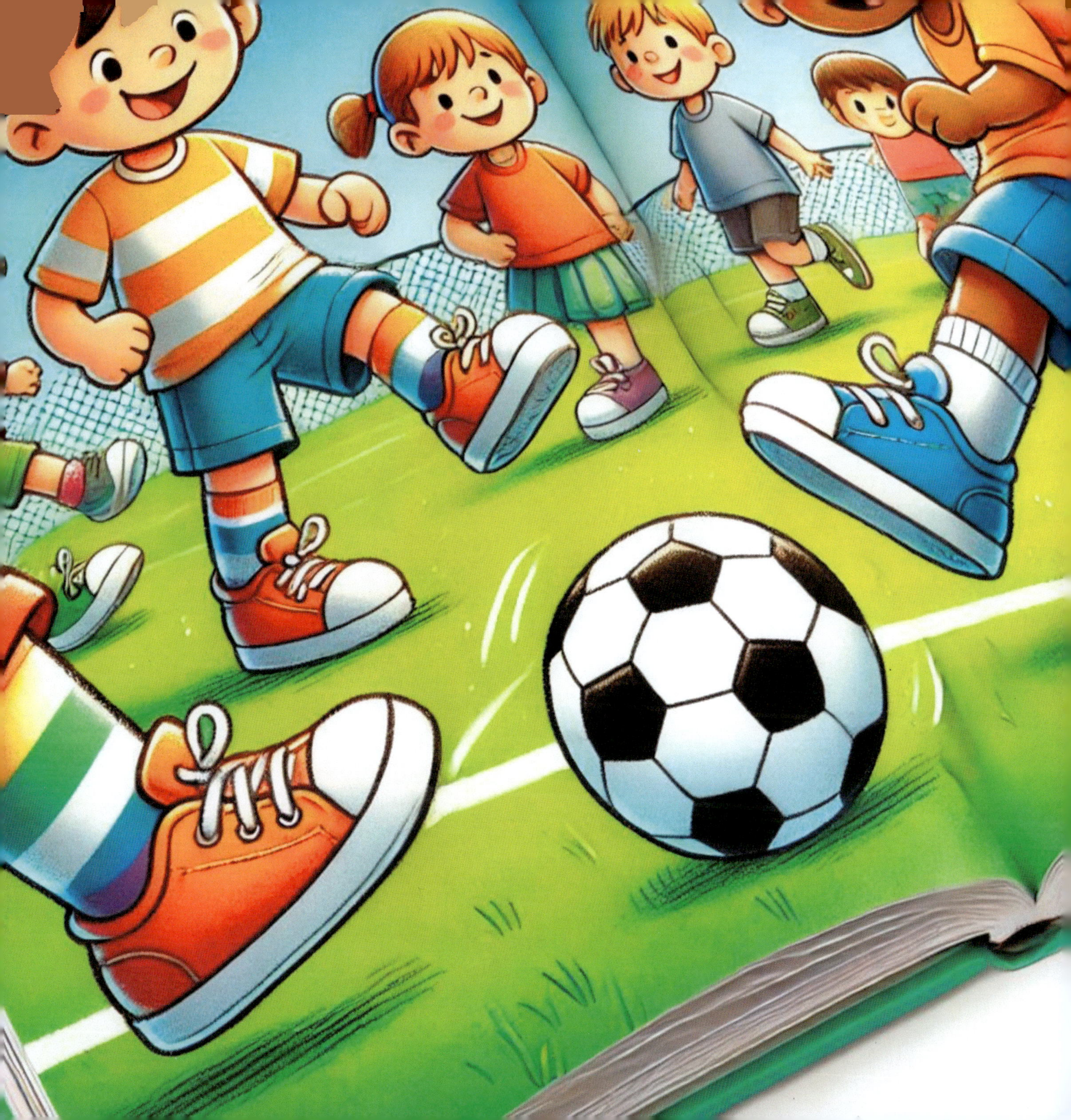

"Let's play!" they say.
"Together, we're strong!"

No matter our color,
we all get along.

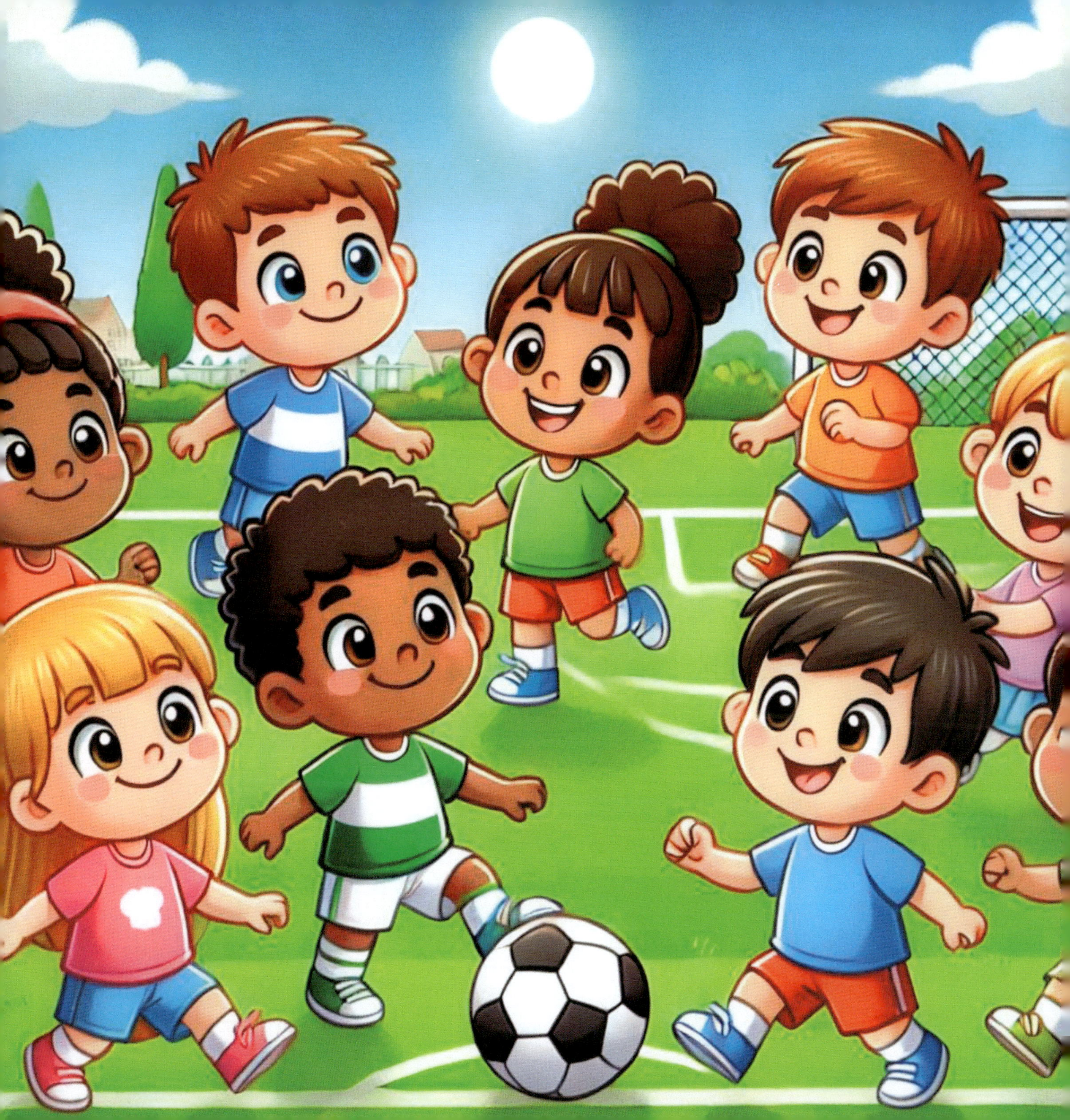

Everyone is welcome,
no matter where you're
from.

Football is fun, and we all
have won!

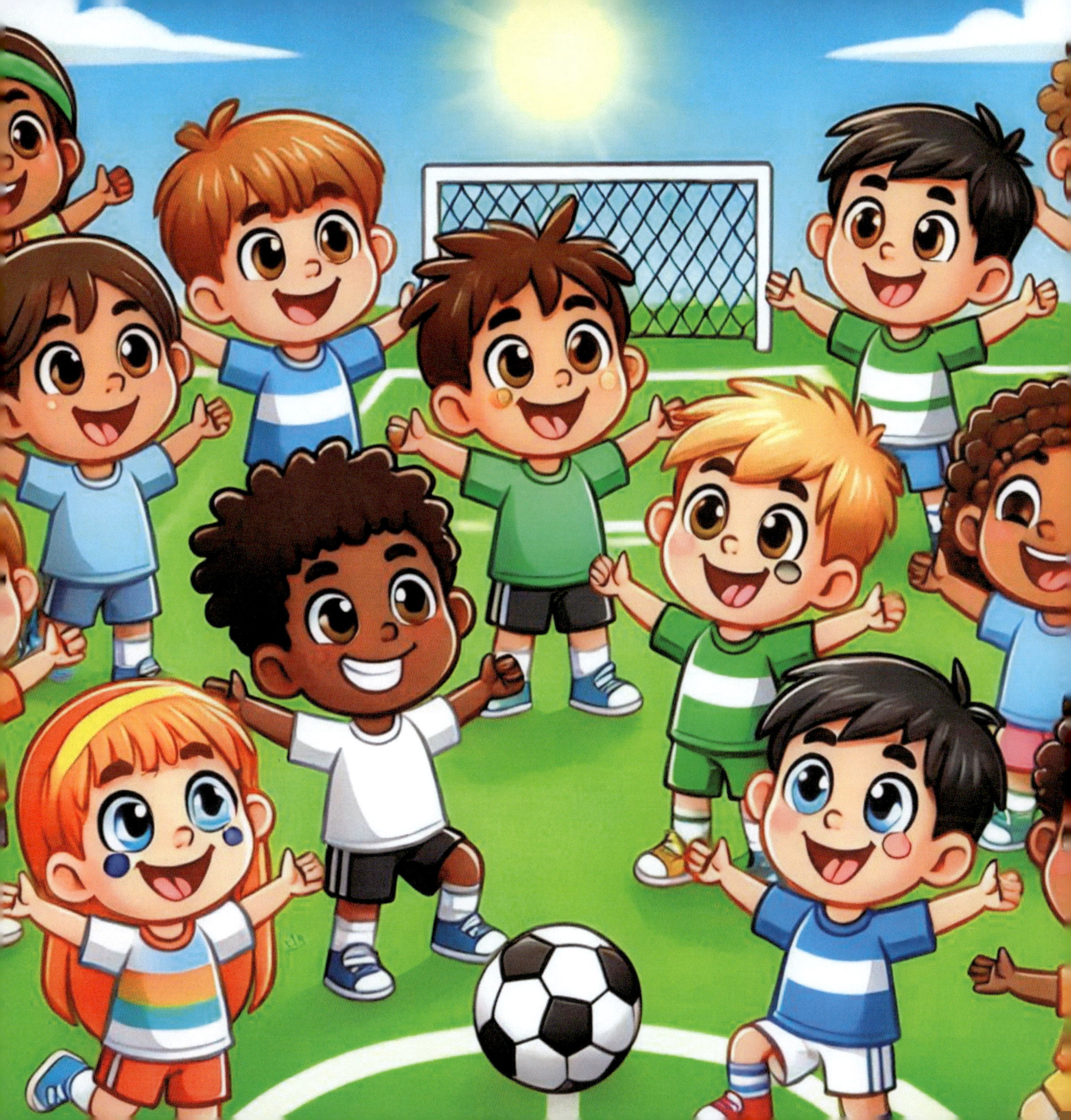

With every kick,
we learn something new.

Football is a language for
me and you!

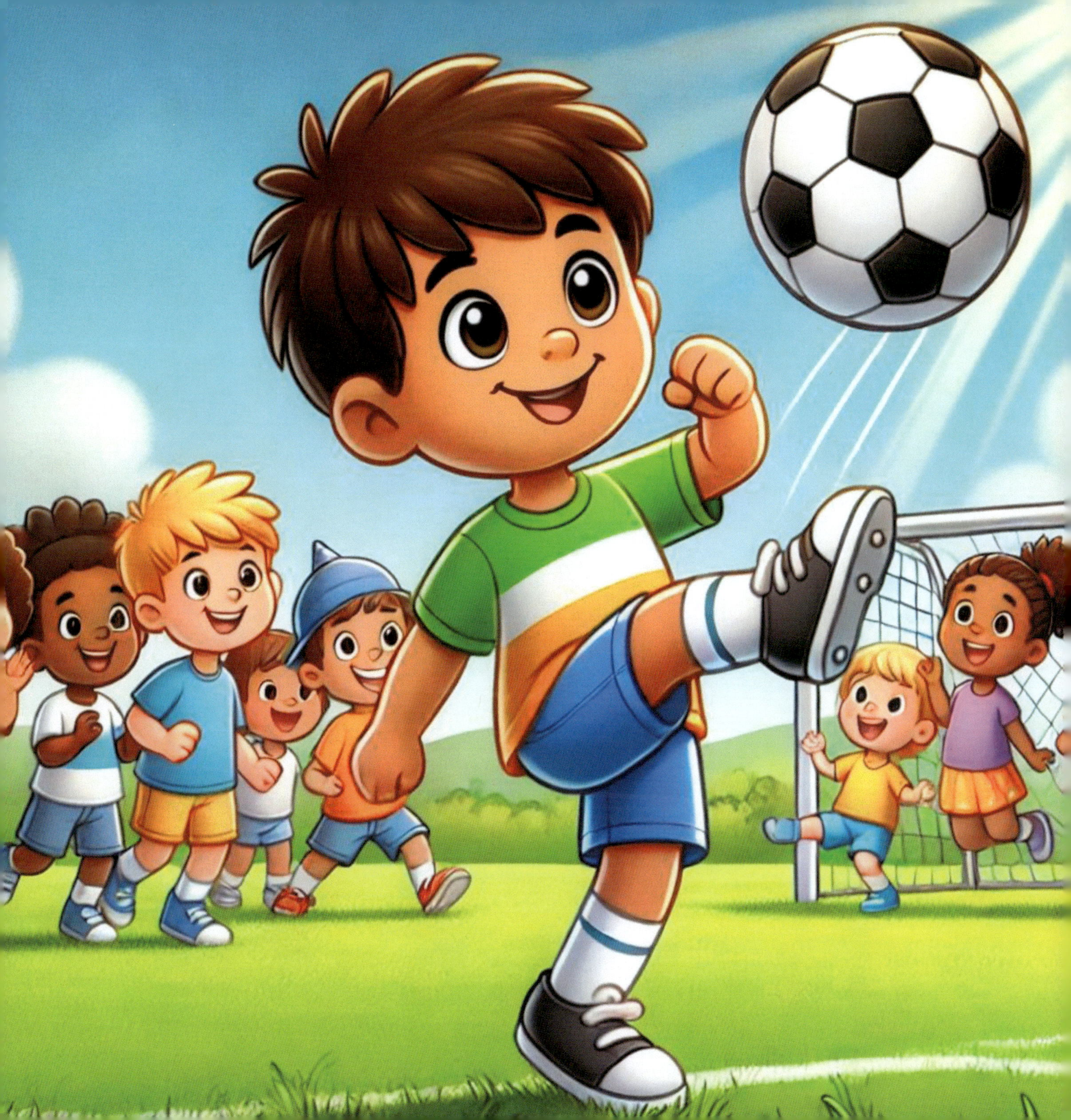

So come, let's play—
together as friends.

In football, the fun never ends!

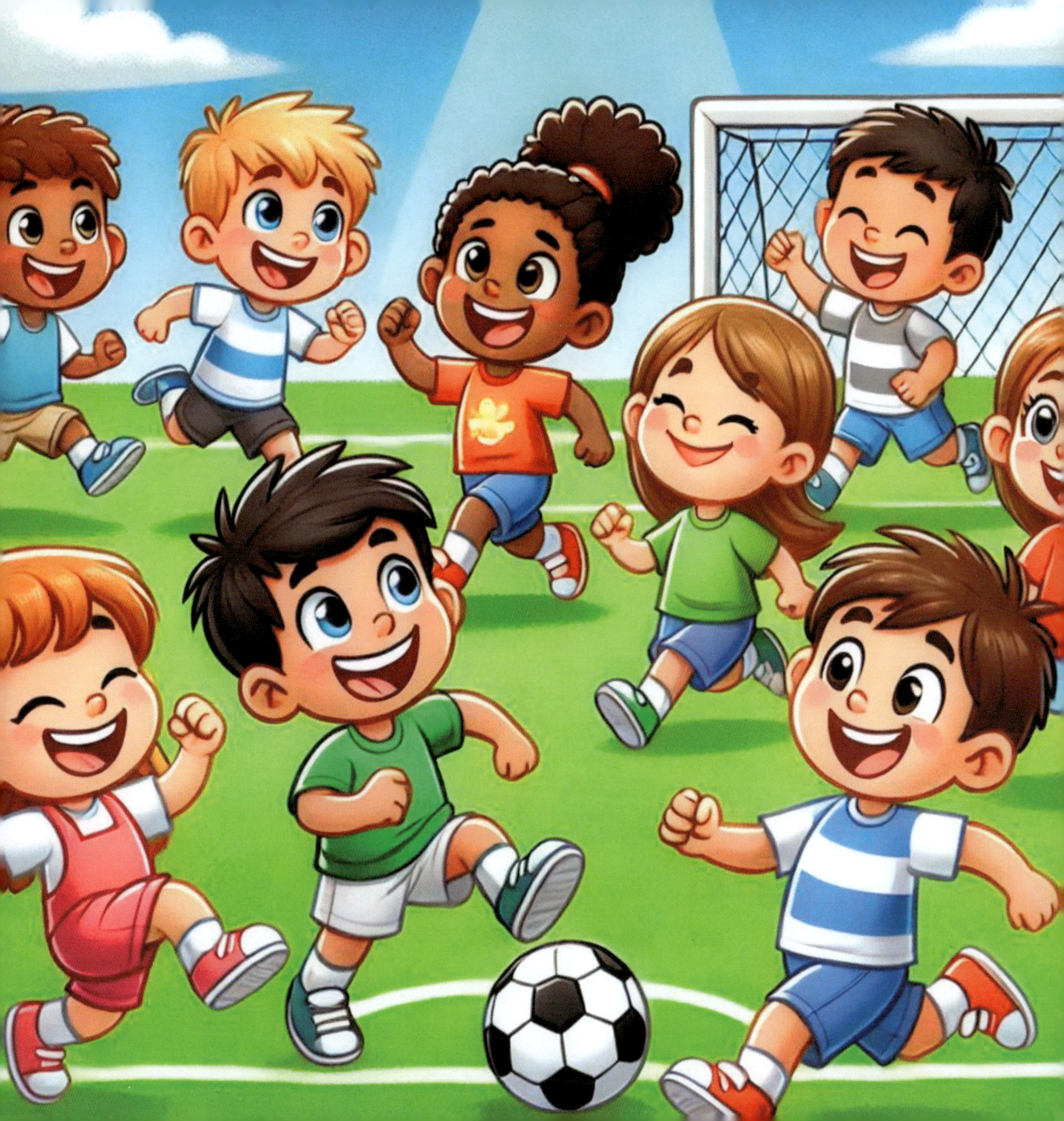

Different faces, one big team,

Playing football is a shared dream!

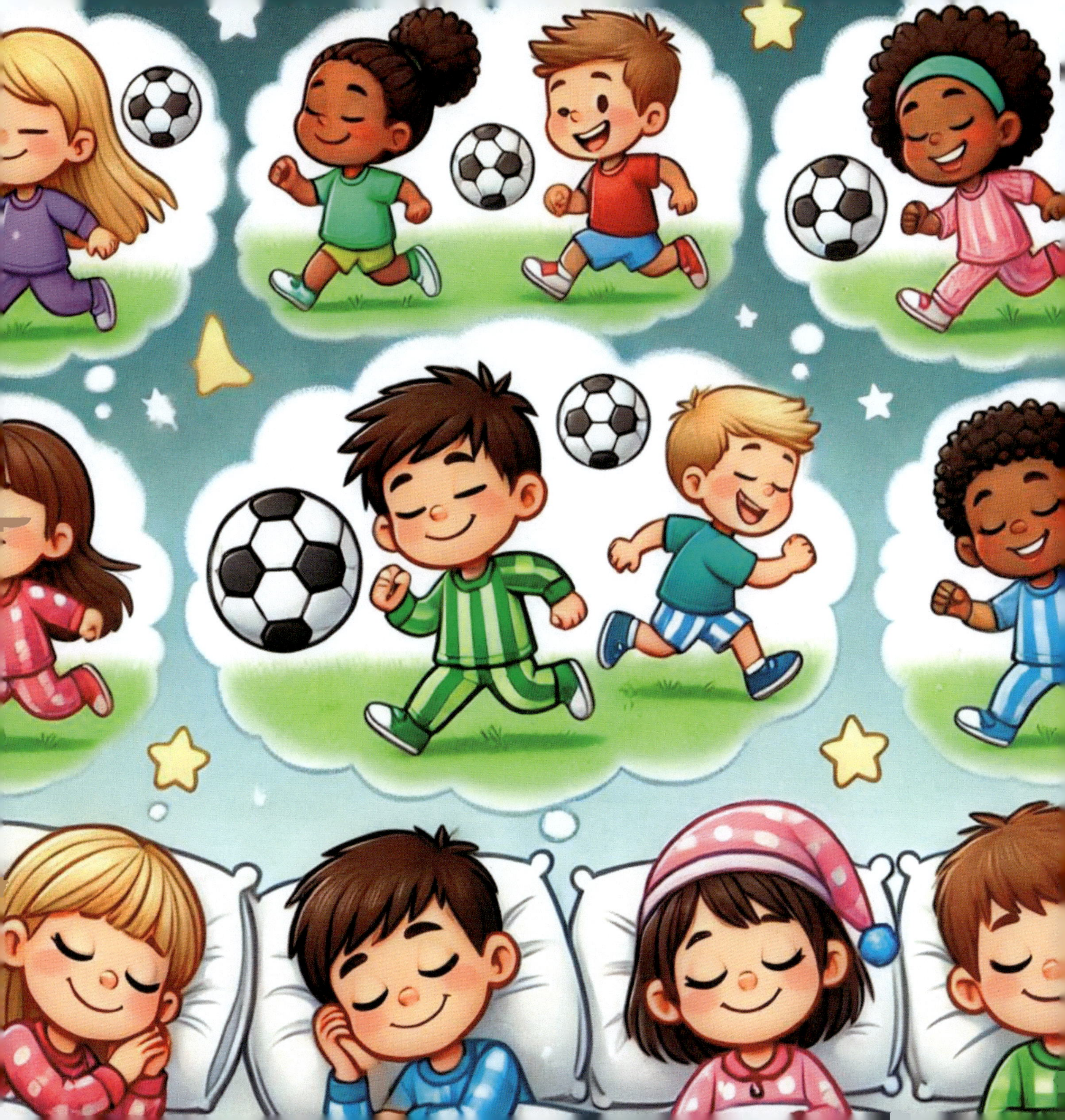

We laugh, we run, we kick with care.

Football is love that we all share!

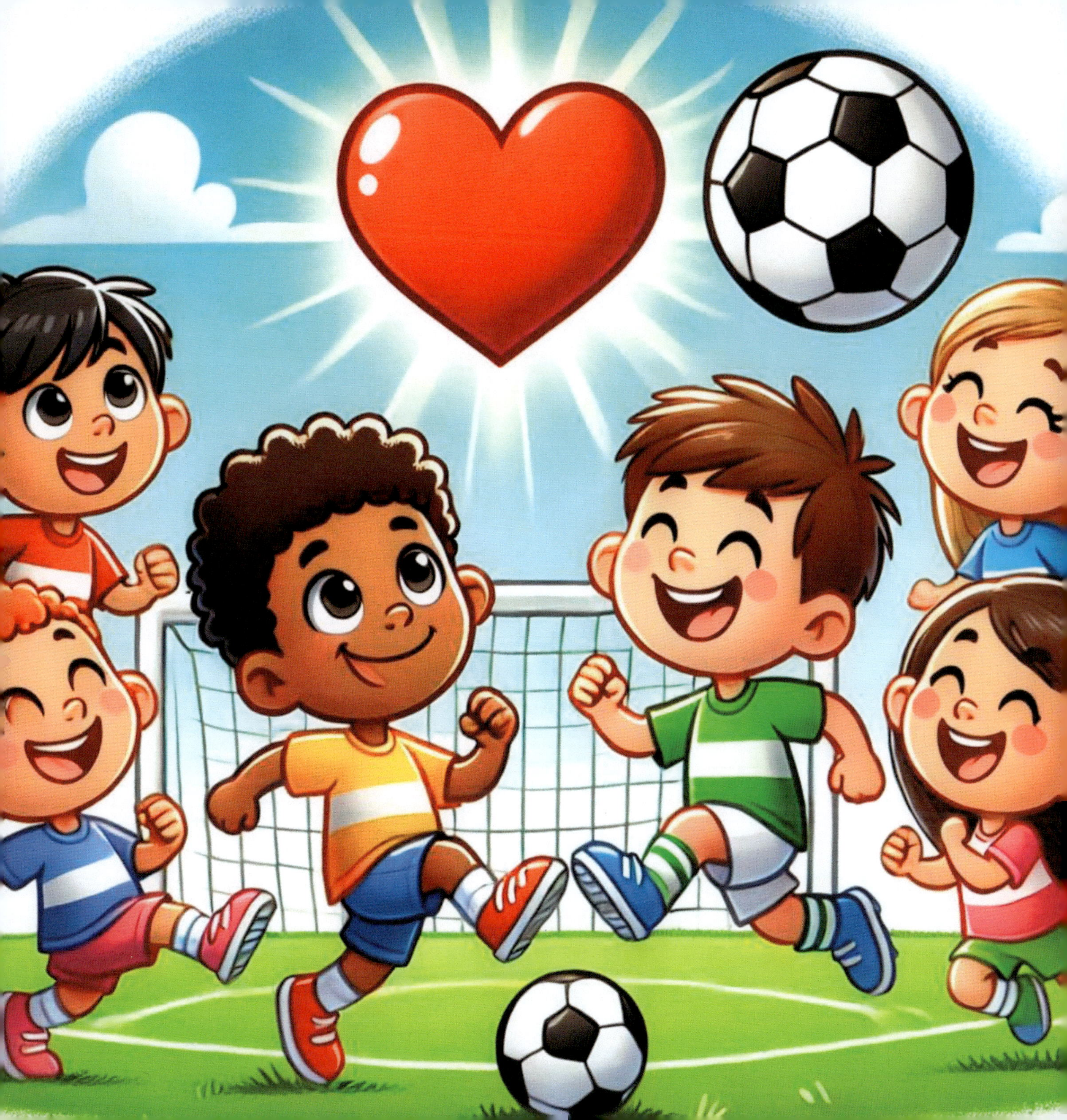

Printed in Great Britain
by Amazon